EASTER SPEECHES AND POEMS

A COLLECTION OF BEAUTIULLY INSPIRED WORDS

By
CHERYL WORSHAM

Copyright © 2023. All rights reserved

The content contained within this book may not be reproduced, duplicated, or transmitted without direct written permission from the author or the publisher.

TABLE OF CONTENTS

EASTER 1

KNOW MY REDEEMER LIVES 3

JESUS 4

THE CROSS 5

NEVER ALONE 6

RESURRECTION SUNDAY 7

HE'S RISEN FOR ME 8

LET'S CELEBRATE 9

SWEET RESURRECTION 10

WHAT CAN WASH AWAY MY SINS? 12

HE ROSE 13

JESUS IS ALIVE 14

PURE STRENGTH 15

SAY YES TO JESUS 16

PARADISE AWAITS 17

THE VICTORY IS WON 18

LEAN INTO JESUS 19

HIS LOVE 20

PRAISE HIM 21

LET US SHOW UP 22

THE MISSION 23

BEYOND INNOCENCE 24

ETERNAL TEMPLE 25

BULLETPROOF BLESSINGS 27

GLORIOUS SKIES 28

BELOVED KISS 29

THE GREAT PROMISE 30

GENTLE HARVEST 31

MORNING ALTER 32

WONDROUS GIFT 33

THAT SPECIAL LAND 34

EASTER

E is for everlasting life. For God so loved the world that he gave his only begotten son, that whosoever believes in him shall not perish, but have everlasting life. This is the hope we can find in Easter; a hope of resurrection and redemption that is greater than any sorrow we may experience.

A is for Atonement. Easter is a time for reflecting on the atoning sacrifice of Jesus, and how he gave his life for us so that we might live with him in glory.

S is for Salvation. Easter is a reminder of the power of God's grace and love. It is a sign of his mercy and forgiveness, and it is a promise that death does not have the final word.

S is for Transformation. Easter brings with it an opportunity for transformation; to put away our old selves and become new creations in Christ.

E is for Eternal Hope. Easter brings an eternal hope of life, love, and joy that can never be taken away from us. It is a reminder that no matter what trials or tribulations we may face, God will always be with us and guide us to a better tomorrow.

R is for Renewal. Easter is a time for spiritual renewal when we take time to pause and reflect on the incredible gift of salvation that God has given us.

This Easter is an opportunity to rediscover the hope and power of Jesus' resurrection. May you be encouraged to face life's challenges with faith, joy, and confidence in the Lord's enduring love and mercy.

A COLLECTION OF BEAUTIULLY INSPIRED WORDS

KNOW MY REDEEMER LIVES

I know my Redeemer lives, and ever watches over me;

His loving-kindness he daily shows, without ceasing, faithfully.

Though all earthly comforts fail, his presence never fades away;

His grace doth lead me through dark vale, and bless me ev'ry day!

JESUS

J is for Jesus.

E is for Eternity.

S is for Sacrifice.

U is for Unconditional Love.

S is for Salvation.

This Easter, let us remember that Jesus died so that we may have eternal life, and He rose again to demonstrate the power of unconditional love and sacrifice. May we be filled with hope as we reflect on His infinite mercy and grace toward us Amen.

A COLLECTION OF BEAUTIULLY INSPIRED WORDS

THE CROSS

The Cross of Jesus of Nazerath

Is the symbol of His love

It speaks of our relationship with Him

From Heaven, high above

So, this Easter, I pray that you'll come to know

The redeeming power of grace

That we may be transformed by His love

And find hope in each obstacle we face

NEVER ALONE

No matter how dark our days may be

We are never truly alone

For Christ is always by our side

His presence is our own

This Easter, may you trust in Him

That you'll rest in His embrace

No matter the trial or the test to come

He will never leave us nor forsake

A COLLECTION OF BEAUTIULLY INSPIRED WORDS

RESURRECTION SUNDAY

There is room at the cross for you

As we gather this Resurrection Sunday

Let us rejoice in Christ's victory over death

And the hope and joy our salvation brings

May your Easter be filled with peace, grace and love

Knowing that nothing can separate us from the power of his His love

HE'S RISEN FOR ME
(Sing to the tune of "Jesus Loves Me")

On Calvery's cross, He died for me.

His love's a river, flowing free.

I'm so glad my savior lives. Eternal life He freely gives.

Chorus

He's risen' for me!

He's risen' for me!

He's risen' for me!

For the Bible says it's so!

Verse 2

Sing hallelujah, to my Lord!

Abundant life is our reward!

Chorus

He's Risen for me!

He's Risen for me! He's Risen for Me!

For the Bible says it's so!

LET'S CELEBRATE

Let's take a moment to reflect and see

What Easter means for you and me

It's a time of rebirth, renewal and joy

It's an occasion that we should all enjoy

Let this Easter bring you peace and delight

For this is an opportunity to make things right

As we come together to celebrate God's dear son

Let's never forget what we he has done

May Easter be a reminder of all that is good

And may we each seek to do all that we should

So, let's have an Easter full of love and cheer

Wishing you joy happiness and a blessed year!

Happy Easter!

SWEET RESURRECTION

This Easter message requires a poster board, candy and gum wrappers, scissors, glue, permanent marker, Lifesavers, Mounds, M&Ms, Now and Later, Snickers, Lollipop, Jellybeans, and Extra.

*** *You will find the word Lollipop on a box of Jolly Rancher Lollipops.*

Step 1: Copy the Easter Message template on poster board leaving space for the wrappers. Make sure to leave enough space between each word for the wrappers.

Step 2: Remove the candy and gum from the wrapper.

Step 3: Trim the edges of the wrappers as needed.

Step 4: Place each wrapper onto the poster board and glue it down.

Step 5: Outline each wrapper with a permanent marker for emphasis.

Your message made from candy bar wrappers is now complete!

Enjoy!

Dear Lord,

You are a LIFESAVER.

We owe our lives to you.

We study MOUNDS of scripture and learn of all you do.

And just like M&Ms, your love's so smooth and sweet.

We honor you NOW and LATER for your mercy and grace we'll eat.

Though there were many ungrateful SNICKERS when they nailed you to the cross.

Your LOLLIPOP sweet love never failed us at such great cost.

So, let's raise our JELLYBEANS in honor of our Lord today.

For his EXTRA special love and the price that he did pay.

WHAT CAN WASH AWAY MY SINS?

What can wash away my sins

The blood of Jesus

What can make me whole again

Nothing but the blood of Jesus

We thank HIM for the gift of Easter

Which gives us a hope from above

That we can live a life apart from sin

With the grace of God's perfect love

We live a life of joy

Of His mercy and His grace

Let us all celebrate this Easter

And give our Lord the praise

A COLLECTION OF BEAUTIULLY INSPIRED WORDS

HE ROSE

Toddler 1: And on the third Day

Toddler 2: He Rose

Toddler 3: With all Power

Toddler 4: In His Hands

All toddlers sing as children walk toward the group singing (to the tune of "Ten Little Indians")

One little, two little

three little Christians,

Four little,

Five little

Six little Christians,

Seven little,

Eight little

Nine little Christians,

Ten little Christians were born.

Happy Easter!

JESUS IS ALIVE

J is for Jesus. He is our risen King.

E is for Eternity. He's our everything.

S is for Salvation. We're no longer dead in sin.

U is for Unconditional love. It will never end.

S is for Security. He's our strength and hope.

I is for Immortality and life beyond the scope.

S is for his Selflessness. He gave us all he had.

A is for Atonement. Forgiveness, we are glad.

L is for Love that He gave from Calvary's tree.

I is for Invitation of life eternity.

V is for the Victory. It's ours in Jesus name.

E is for Everlasting life. Forever we will claim.

PURE STRENGTH

Where is the strength that comes from within?

It lies in Jesus, who washed away our sin.

He commands us to stand and always be brave,

For He is the one who fights our battles and He is the one who saves.

May we all be blessed this Easter, as our Lord lives on high.

Let us rejoice with love and grace, for His resurrection is nigh!

He has a place for us where the streets are paved with gold.

We can find joy in the promise of eternity, for our God is mighty and bold.

Happy Easter! May you feel His everlasting love and power within your heart Amen.

SAY YES TO JESUS

Yes, He's the only way.

Yes, He is our hope today.

Yes, He's the one who saves.

Yes, He conquered death and the grave.

Yes, We will forever sing

Of our Holy risen King.

He has conquered sin and shame

By the power of His name.

Say Yes to Jesus on this Easter Day.

In our hearts, He'll forever stay.

Happy Easter everyone!! May the Lord bless and keep you throughout this season and always Amen.

PARADISE AWAITS

Paradise awaits us, in Heaven, we will see

A place where love abounds, for us eternally

The streets are paved with gold; the jewels are made of light

A place where we can live forever oh so precious in His sight

Let us celebrate this Easter, so glorious and so grand

For Jesus tasted death for us, on the cross He did stand

He gave his life as a ransom, that we may be set free

The hope of eternity is ours through His death on Calvary

THE VICTORY IS WON

He has won the victory, over death and sin

The angels sing for joy, His love will never end

He rose from the tomb in glorious splendor that morn

And opened the gates of Heaven, forever to adorn

We give praise to our Lord; His mercy is so grand

Let us all rejoice in His victory over evil's ugly hand

This Easter, let us remember and keep Him near our hearts

Because of Him death has no sting- all sorrow do depart

Happy Easter to all of you! May the Lord grant you peace and grace Amen.

LEAN INTO JESUS

Let us lean into Jesus and trust in His might

His love is like a river that runs so deep and bright

It reaches to our hearts and brings life anew

So, let's rejoice, this Easter Day, for all that He can do

Let us kneel in reverence and thank Him for His Grace

For restoration of our souls destined to a better place

So, let us lift our voices and shout with gratitude

Happy Easter, everyone! May His love be your fortitude.

HIS LOVE

Jesus, our King of love, is risen and divine

His power extends far beyond the boundaries of time

He died for the sins of man but rose from the dead

Bestowing upon us His grace, mercy, and peace instead

He brought us salvation and hope and love that will never end

And it is in Him that we can find true strength and life, again

His love is incomparable and no other can compare

To the love our Lord has for us, with His mercy and His care

This Easter season, let us be thankful for all that He has done

His grace and mercy will be with us, until the race is run

PRAISE HIM

He is our Lord and Saviour, the one who sets us free

His grace and mercy guide us on this Easter day we see

The empty grave of darkness has shone the light of love

So, we could walk in freedom of His goodness from above

His power will never cease to be and His love shall never part

For our Lord and God watches over us, with a love that's in our heart

This Easter, let us all lift up our voices and give the Lord our praise

For without Him we'd have nothing, let's glorify His name today

LET US SHOW UP

Let us show up for Jesus, our voices loud and clear

To sing all praises to our Lord, His love we will revere

For Jesus conquered death on that early Easter morn

By sacrificing Himself for us, so we may be reborn

Our steps are ordered in His way, a pathway so divine

He watches over us and guides us, so sublime

So, let us show up today and give to Him our love

For in Him alone is hope and mercy from above

A COLLECTION OF BEAUTIULLY INSPIRED WORDS

THE MISSION

On this glorious Easter morn, let us rejoice and sing

Our Lord has conquered death, and our peace bells they ring

The grave could no longer keep Him bound, for He rose up so true

The mission was completed, and our hearts were made anew.

Let us strive to do His work, and follow his command

For He has given us the power to take a brand-new stand

The Lord will always be with us, we need not ever fear

His grace and mercy guiding us, forever drawing near.

So, let us keep our gaze upon Him, and spread His love to all

Let us be living examples of His Light, so that none on earth may fall

Let us honor Him with our deeds, so all the world may see

The beauty of Jesus Christ in us and follow Him faithfully.

BEYOND INNOCENCE

He gives us hope when innocence was gone

A chance to start anew with each new dawn

He conquered death and gave us the power

To rise beyond the darkest hour

He died for us in love so true

Rising again in morning dew

His mission here on earth was done

But the love He gave still lives on

Let us not give up on Him

Our God who lightens every whim

He is the answer all our prayers

Granting us peace in times of despair

Let us be thankful for what second chances bring

As we bask in His glory and praises, we will sing!

Happy Easter everyone! May the Lord bless you all this day Amen.

ETERNAL TEMPLE

Cradled in the warmth of His grace

He gave us all a chance to embrace

The gift of mercy and heavenly love

From the eternal example above

We all can experience a special place

In the temple of His everlasting grace

It is here where our faith will forever abide

And through Him it shall never hide

He fills us with hope and joy anew

His presence everlasting and true

He opens our eyes for us to see

His plan and purpose for eternity

Abide in Him and He in you

No matter what you may go through

You will never walk alone

Your faith and love shall both grow strong

Through our Lord Jesus we shall forever be free

Let us celebrate His eternal love and great mercy

BULLETPROOF BLESSINGS

He gifted us the strength for life,

A shield of faith to battle strife.

The power of His love, a mighty sword,

Defending us from the enemy's horde.

He sends His grace in overflowing measure,

A blessing of love to last forever.

His mercy, justice, and unshakable trust,

Will provide us with a sure and solid thrust.

Through His love, we have become bulletproof,

Protected in battle by His mighty truth.

No weapon formed against us shall ever succeed,

For our Lord is alive and will always lead.

He guards us with peace and strength divine,

Rich blessings that we may never decline.

So, when life throws punches in the air,

Just remember Jesus is always there.

GLORIOUS SKIES

Glorious skies on high stretch blue and clear,

The heavens declare God's majesty here.

A gentle whisper of our Lord's delight,

Meant to fill us with his strength and might.

As we look up at that glorious sky,

Let us remember that Easter is why.

Our Savior Jesus died to cleanse our sins,

And from death rose up with strength within.

Let us be humble and accept God's plan

And give thanks for his sacrifice, however grand.

Let us remember his resurrection each day-

That he rose again and showed us the way!

BELOVED KISS

Toddler 1: Beloved Kiss

Toddler 2: Of Mercy and Grace

Toddler 3: A gift of love

Toddler 4: We cannot replace

Toddler 1: Happy Easter

Toddler 2: To one and all

Toddler 3: Let us live

Toddler 4: By His call

THE GREAT PROMISE

He rose again on Easter morn

A promise that we can be reborn

From death and darkness, we have been freed

For Jesus gave us a brand-new creed

He has given us the power to live again

To feel joy and peace within

The price of freedom he did pay

So that each of us could have a brighter day

This is the blessing of Easter, our Lord's great grace

Let us all accept it with humble embrace

Happy Easter everyone! May the Lord bless you all this day Amen.

GENTLE HARVEST

Gentle harvest of our Lord's abiding grace,

A blessing that we can never replace.

His love and mercy have no bounds,

Our lives with joy and his peace surrounds.

The price of freedom was paid one day,

As Jesus Christ gave His life away.

He conquered death and its mighty hold,

All power in His hands will ever unfold.

Let us remember Him on this sweet Easter Day,

His resurrection and the joy it brings our way.

MORNING ALTER

The sweet morning alters of His amazing grace,

A gift of love that we can never replace.

He gave us the power to stand strong and tall,

To have faith and not fear life's wretched fall.

Let us honour Him on this beautiful Easter Day,

For He has shown us a brighter more acceptable way.

Through His amazing grace and perfect will,

The abundant life we will fulfill.

WONDROUS GIFT

The wondrous gift of our Lord's love

A blessing sent from Heaven above

On Easter Day let us remember Him

The joy of His resurrection, a blessing never dim

His perfect love has given us all life's grace

Allowing us to live in this blessed place

Let us honour Him with our thanksgiving song

For the gift of His love can never be wrong

We love Him more and more each day

Our Lord and Saviour, Jesus Christ is the Way!

THAT SPECIAL LAND

That special land where Jesus stands,

A place of love with outstretched hands.

The glory of His resurrection day,

Bringing hope and joy in a better way.

We are bound together with His love divine,

Through the power of His grace and mercy combined.

Let us honour Him on this Easter Day,

With all our hearts and in every way.

So, let us rejoice in all that we've been given,

And thank God for such a beautiful risen--- Lord!

Happy Easter to you all! Amen.

Made in the USA
Coppell, TX
16 March 2025